Intermediate 1
# English

**2004 Exam**
Close Reading
Critical Essay

**2005 Exam**
Close Reading
Critical Essay

**2006 Exam**
Close Reading
Critical Essay

**2007 Exam**
Close Reading
Critical Essay

**2008 Exam**
Close Reading
Critical Essay

Leckie×Leckie

© Scottish Qualifications Authority
All rights reserved. Copying prohibited. No part of this publication may be reproduced, stored in a retrieval system, or transmitted in any form or by any means, electronic, mechanical, photocopying, recording or otherwise.

First exam published in 2004.
Published by Leckie & Leckie Ltd, 3rd Floor, 4 Queen Street, Edinburgh EH2 1JE
tel: 0131 220 6831 fax: 0131 225 9987 enquiries@leckieandleckie.co.uk www.leckieandleckie.co.uk

ISBN 978-1-84372-650-0

A CIP Catalogue record for this book is available from the British Library.

Leckie & Leckie is a division of Huveaux plc.

Leckie & Leckie is grateful to the copyright holders, as credited at the back of the book, for permission to use their material.
Every effort has been made to trace the copyright holders and to obtain their permission for the use of copyright material.
Leckie & Leckie will gladly receive information enabling them to rectify any error or omission in subsequent editions.

2004 | Intermediate I

[BLANK PAGE]

# X115/101

NATIONAL
QUALIFICATIONS
2004

FRIDAY, 14 MAY
1.00 PM – 1.45 PM

ENGLISH
INTERMEDIATE 1
Close Reading

Answer all questions.

30 marks are allocated to this paper.

Read the passage carefully and then answer **all** the questions, **using your own words where asked to do so.**

The questions will ask you to show that:

you understand **what** the writer has said (main ideas and supporting details) (**Understanding—U**);

you can identify **how** the writer has said it (techniques of structure and style) (**Analysis—A**);

you can comment on **how well** the writer has achieved his purpose (using appropriate evidence) (**Evaluation—E**).

A code letter (U, A, E) is used alongside each question to identify its purpose for you.

In the passage which follows, the writer and entertainer Tony Hawks describes his first visit to Ireland and the effect it had on him.

In 1989 I went to Ireland for the first time. I don't know why it had taken so long. Some parts of the world you make a conscious effort to visit and others have to wait until fate delivers you there.

When the moment arrived for me to set foot on the Emerald Isle, it was as a result of a
5 badly written song. An Irish friend from London, Seamus, had urged me to compose a piece for him and his mate Tom to sing at an International Song Competition which was held each year in his home town. Qualification for the final, he explained, was a formality provided I agreed to do a twenty-minute comedy set for the audience whilst the judges were out. Seamus wanted to perform a humorous song, and had asked me
10 to come up with something that would "set it apart" from the other entries. In the event, what would set it apart would be a quite significant drop in standard.

The song I had written was called "I Wanna Have Tea With Batman". Now I consider myself to be a good songwriter, but this song was—how can I put it?—yes, that's it— poor. To their credit, Seamus and Tom conjured up a performance to match it.

15 In an extraordinary gesture which was at best surreal and at worst embarrassing, they dressed as Batman and Robin. At least that's what they had aimed to do, but a limited costume budget had left them in borrowed tights, lycra shorts and academic robes doubling as capes. They resembled a couple of children entered for a fancy dress competition by uninterested parents. Seamus seemed unconcerned, his theory of
20 comedy being that if you had an "outrageous" outfit, that was enough; and *then* he announced his masterstroke—one of them would carry a teapot and the other a kettle!

One had to admire his courage, for he was performing in front of his home town and everyone he had grown up with was there: friends, family, teachers, priests, shopkeepers, barmen and drunks—all were rooting for him. If one was going to let oneself down very
25 badly—and Seamus was most definitely going to do that—it would be difficult to imagine an assembled throng on whom it would have more effect.

Seamus and Tom took centre stage. The audience responded with an audible intake of breath. For them, there was little to suggest that the two characters before them were supposed to be Batman and Robin, and they were clearly taken aback by this magnificent
30 fusion of colour, tights and kitchen appliances.

I watched from the back, experiencing for the first time a curious blend of wonder and discomfort, and could see in the faces of both performers that their self-belief in the costume selection was ebbing away with each long second. Thankfully, the crowd's astonishment melted into applause. The conductor caught the eye of our superheroes
35 and they nodded to establish they were ready.

The band struck up. The musical introduction finished but neither Tom nor Seamus began singing. They looked accusingly at each other. Paralysed with nerves, one of them had missed their cue. Somebody near me allowed their head to drop into their hands. Seamus, man of the moment, stepped forward and signalled to the conductor to stop the
40 band. Astonishingly the maestro ignored him. He was pretending he couldn't see Seamus's frantic signals. How bad could his eyesight be? Was it possible not to notice the flapping arms of a multi-coloured caped crusader brandishing a teapot in anger?

That conductor was more focused than most of us could ever hope to be. He had a long evening to get through and he was going to get through it in the shortest available time. Going back and starting again for those who had screwed up wasn't on the agenda, even if it was "good old Seamus" from down the road. And so, with all the obstinacy of a First World War general, his head stayed firmly down and the band played on.

Time stood still.

I simply have no way of knowing how long it was before Seamus abandoned his frenzied gesticulations, punched Tom, and they both began singing. Indeed, I can't recall how badly they performed the rest of the song. Who cares? The audience applauded, they won "Most Entertaining Act", and so began my fascination with Ireland.

*Adapted from* Round Ireland with a Fridge *by Tony Hawks*

## QUESTIONS

*Marks Code*

1. In the opening paragraph (lines 1–3), the writer gives two different explanations for visiting "parts of the world".

   **In your own words** say what they are.     2   U

2. The writer's visit to Ireland was as a result of an invitation to write a song for his friends.

   What else did he have to do to ensure that they would qualify for the final of the Competition?

   **Answer in your own words**.     2   U

3. (*a*) **In your own words** describe fully the kind of song Seamus asked the writer "to come up with" (line 10).     2   U

   (*b*) **In your own words** explain what, according to the writer, actually "set it apart" from the others.     2   U

4. By referring to examples from lines 12–14, explain how the writer's **word choice** and **punctuation** help to create an informal, conversational tone.     4   A

5. "They resembled a couple of children . . . uninterested parents" (lines 18–19).

   How does this comparison help to show that Seamus's and Tom's costumes were not very good?     2   A

6. Why do you think the writer describes carrying a teapot and kettle as Seamus's "masterstroke" (line 21)?     2   A

7. Look again at lines 22–26.

   The writer feels that one "had to admire" Seamus's courage.

   Explain how any **one feature of the sentence structure** in lines 22–24 helps to convey this feeling.     2   A

Marks Code

8. Look again at lines 27–33.

    "Seamus and Tom took centre stage" (line 27).

    **In your own words, explain fully:**

    (a) **how** the audience reacted at first;     1 U

    (b) **how** the writer felt as he "watched from the back";     2 U

    (c) **what** Seamus and Tom were beginning to think.     2 U

9. Comment on the effectiveness of the writer's use of **word choice or sentence structure** in creating tension in lines 36–42.     2 E

10. "Time stood still" (line 48).

    Identify any **two techniques** the writer uses to emphasise this idea.     2 A

11. Seamus eventually gave up using "frenzied gesticulations" (lines 49–50).

    Quote an expression used earlier in the passage which helps you to understand this idea.     1 U

12. Look again at lines 51–52.

    Explain how effective you find this final sentence to be as an ending to the passage.     2 E

                                            **Total (30)**

[END OF QUESTION PAPER]

# X115/102

NATIONAL
QUALIFICATIONS
2004

FRIDAY, 14 MAY
2.05 PM – 2.50 PM

ENGLISH
INTERMEDIATE 1
Critical Essay

Answer **one** question only.

Each question is worth 25 marks.

Attempt ONE question only, taken from any of the Sections A to E. Write the number of the question you attempt in the margin of your answer book.

In all Sections you may use Scottish texts.

You should remember:

- your answer should be relevant to the question
- you should check your spelling and punctuation.

## SECTION A—DRAMA

1. Choose a play in which an important character is successful in overcoming a difficulty or solving a problem.

   Say what the difficulty or problem is and show how the character overcomes it by the end of the play.

   In your answer you should refer to such features as: character, plot, or any other appropriate feature.

2. Choose a play in which the characters have to face an issue such as bullying, family problems, racism, or any other issue.

   Say what the issue is and show how successful or unsuccessful one of the characters is in dealing with the issue.

   In your answer you should refer to such features as: theme, character, or any other appropriate feature.

## SECTION B—PROSE

3. Choose a novel **or** a short story which has an important turning point that changes things for one of the characters.

   Show how the story builds up to the turning point and say why it is important for the character.

   In your answer you should refer to such features as: structure, character, or any other appropriate feature.

4. Choose a novel, **or** a short story, **or** a piece of non-fiction, **or** a group of prose texts which deals with a topic of importance to society.

   Say what you learned about the topic from your reading and whether you felt sympathy for the people involved.

   In your answer you should refer to such features as: theme, character, or any other appropriate feature.

## SECTION C—POETRY

5. Choose a poem which focuses on a person's experience.

   Say what the experience is and how the particular words and phrases the poet uses help you to understand how the person feels.

   In your answer you should refer to such features as: word choice, imagery, or any other appropriate feature.

6. Choose a poem which creates a particular mood or atmosphere for you.

   Say what the mood or atmosphere is and go on to show how it is created by the language of the poem.

   In your answer you should refer to such features as: word choice, imagery, sound effects, or any other appropriate feature.

## SECTION D—MASS MEDIA

7. Choose a film or *TV drama which has sequences where special effects are important.

   Describe some of the special effects and say why you found them successful.

   In your answer you should refer to such features as: computer-generated images, animation, or any other appropriate feature.

8. Choose a film or *TV drama which gives a picture of society in Britain today.

   What sort of picture of society does it give? How does it try to make you feel that it is true to life?

   In your answer you should refer to such features as: character, theme, setting, or any other appropriate feature.

   * "TV drama" may be a single play, series or serial.

## SECTION E—LANGUAGE

9. Consider the language that you use in talking to different groups of people.

   What changes have you noticed in your own use of language in at least two different situations? How do you think these changes help you to communicate well with the different groups?

   In your answer you should refer to such features as accent, vocabulary, or any other appropriate feature.

10. Consider the language of advertising in newspapers, or in magazines, or on television, or radio.

    Choose one advertisement and say how successful it is in persuading you to buy the product.

    In your answer you should refer to such features as: word choice, tone, or any other appropriate feature.

*[END OF QUESTION PAPER]*

[BLANK PAGE]

2005 | Intermediate I

[BLANK PAGE]

# X115/101

NATIONAL
QUALIFICATIONS
2005

FRIDAY, 13 MAY
1.00 PM – 1.45 PM

ENGLISH
INTERMEDIATE 1
Close Reading

Answer all questions.

30 marks are allocated to this paper.

Read the passage carefully and then answer **all** the questions, **using your own words where asked to do so**.

The questions will ask you to show that:

you understand **what** the writer has said (main ideas and supporting details) (**Understanding—U**);

you can identify **how** the writer has said it (techniques of structure and style) (**Analysis—A**);

you can comment on **how well** the writer has achieved his purpose (using appropriate evidence) (**Evaluation—E**).

A code letter (U, A, E) is used alongside each question to identify its purpose for you.

*In this extract the writer, Blake Morrison, revisits the village in which he grew up and meets 12 year old Daniel Proctor.*

## CHILDREN OF THE DALES

At first glance, Daniel Proctor's bedroom looks pretty much what you'd expect. There are posters of Andy Cole and the fixture list for the football season. There are photos of the England rugby team and a gleaming red Ferrari. There's a globe on the window sill, with a switch to illuminate it. There's a model tank, and a heap of lolly sticks. There aren't many books I can see, but then twelve-year olds like Daniel are said not to read much any more. What did I think I'd find? The Famous Five?

There is no computer in Daniel's bedroom, but his big brother Thomas has one in his, an Amiga, and there's also a Game Boy in the house somewhere. Daniel's favourite computer games are football games; then what he calls beat-'em-up games, like Mortal Kombat 2, with special moves; then shooting games, like Better Archery. He doesn't have a television in his room yet, but he might when he's older, like Thomas. He doesn't mind because there's one downstairs he can watch. Saturday, he says, is the best night for television.

A few minutes ago, Daniel came home in his school uniform. Now he's wearing blue socks, Bermuda shorts and a red T-shirt that says BLOGGS/JOE BLOGGS across the chest. His trainers are downstairs, by the back door, ready and waiting for when we're done talking and he can get out on his bicycle.

But I'm lingering in his bedroom, which—now I come to look at it more closely—seems rather less stereotypical. That model tank, for instance: Daniel made it himself, not from an Airfix kit, but at school, in a design and technology class. And those lolly sticks aren't just scattered at random, but form the roof of another model he made, of a house. There are other things Daniel has made here: clay pots, an ugly mug, and a wooden balancing toy. He's more animated talking about them than he is pointing out the sports posters—which are, on examination, oddly dated: the football fixture list is for the 1993–4 season, and that England rugby team goes back to 1991.

I ask Daniel if he reads much. Yes, he says. What sort of thing? At the moment he's reading Robert Louis Stevenson—*Treasure Island* and *Kidnapped*. He used to read Roald Dahl—oh, and all the Famous Five books, when he was younger. Do I know them? he asks. They're by Enid Blyton.

Daniel looks eager to be off outside. He can't show me his chicken run, he says, because it's a bit of a way off, in a small croft, but we could look at his greenhouse, which is right outside. *His* greenhouse? Yes, when he was seven he was given a growing kit: sunflower seeds, pea seeds, lettuce seeds. It gave him a taste for horticulture: seeing things shoot up like that, from nothing. So for his tenth birthday, he asked for a greenhouse. That bed of potatoes there, where his mother's roses used to be, is also his. You've got to be careful to earth potatoes, he tells me—that means building the earth up over them, because otherwise, if they get above ground, they go green and poisonous. As for the chickens, he incubated them in the house, kept them for a week after they'd hatched under a lamp, then once they'd got a few feathers moved them outside. He feeds them each morning before going to school: he lifts the little hatch and they run out and sometimes jump up on him for bread. Then he collects the dozen or so eggs the hens have laid.

I ask if he gets a weekly comic. No. But he did used to get *Poultry News*.

I have a particular interest in Daniel, because I grew up in the same place and
went to the same schools. My parents were doctors, not farmers, and our house,
though a little aloof from the village, was not set in such splendid isolation as
Daniel's farm. But I walked the same paths, literally—and even had one or two of
the same teachers.

Looking at Daniel's upbringing, and comparing it with mine, I wanted to
understand some of the obvious ways in which childhood has changed in the past
thirty years—and some of the less obvious ways in which it hasn't. In particular, I
wanted to test the theory that today's kids, wherever and however they're raised,
grow up much faster than we did—are rougher, edgier, more knowing and
derisive.

Yet there's little in the manner of Daniel, or of his brothers, to suggest this:
they're bright, responsive, friendly, talkative—even, by all accounts, when not
required to put on a show for a stranger like me. When I ask Daniel about his
television habits, he says his favourite soaps are *Coronation Street*—"everyone
watches that round here"—and *EastEnders*: otherwise games shows and films, if
there's a good one on—something like *Ghostbusters 2*, *Gremlins 2*, the Indiana
Jones films, *The Addams Family* and *Addams Family Values*. Nothing too
different here from the diet of *Emergency Ward Ten* and *Z Cars* which I consumed
at that age.

Does he borrow videos? Occasionally. Or see videos at friends' houses? Yes, he
saw one at Laurence Edmondson's when he slept over there, which he has now
done five times. Has he ever seen a 15-certificate film? He seems a bit vague. I
explain or remind him about 12s and 15s and 18s and PGs. "Yes, I think we're
seeing one at school at the moment. It's called *Macbeth*, and we're reading the
play by William Shakespeare. That's the only one."

For Daniel the world of play means Amiga, Nintendo, Game Boy, Robocop. In
my day, it was Dinky toys, Meccano, Scalextric, Subbuteo and Hornby train sets.
A generation or two earlier and it might have been spinning tops, wooden hoops
and trolleys knocked together from old pram wheels and orange boxes. It's hard
to see that much has been lost. In terms of intellectual stimulus, something may
even have been gained.

Adapted from the essay *Children of the Dales* by Blake Morrison

## QUESTIONS

*Marks Code*

1. The writer says that the bedroom "looks pretty much what you'd expect"(line 1). Give **two** pieces of evidence from lines 1–6 which show this. — 2 U

2. Look again at lines 7–13.

   Quote **two** expressions which suggest that having a Game Boy and his own television are not very important to Daniel. — 2 A

3. Look again at lines 14–19.

   (*a*) What contrast between the writer and Daniel is indicated by the word "But" (line 18)? — 2 U

   (*b*) Why does the writer use the dashes in line 18? — 1 A

4. Look again at lines 18–25.

   (*a*) Quote the expression which shows that perhaps Daniel's bedroom is not as conventional as the writer first thought. — 1 A

   (*b*) By referring in detail to **one** example, show how the writer illustrates that his bedroom is slightly unusual for a teenage boy. — 2 A

5. Explain what the writer is suggesting when he says that Daniel is "more animated talking about them than he is pointing out the sports posters" (lines 23–24). — 2 U

6. What tone is created by the use of italics in *His* (line 32)? — 1 A

7. By referring to **one** example from lines 30–42 show how the writer's **word choice** demonstrates that Daniel is knowledgeable about one of his hobbies. — 2 A

8. Look again at lines 44–48.

   Give **two** similarities and **two** differences between the writer's childhood and Daniel's childhood. — 4 U

9. Explain, **in your own words**, what "theory" the writer "wanted to test" (line 52). — 3 U

10. Why does the writer use the word "Yet" at the start of the paragraph (line 55)? — 1 A

11. Explain the writer's use of italics in lines 58–62. — 1 A

12. How does the **structure** of the sentences in lines 64–69 help to give the reader information about Daniel? — 2 A

13. The writer makes use of humour in this passage. With reference to **one** example comment on how effective you find this technique. — 2 E

14. Explain fully how effective you consider the final paragraph to be in summing up the writer's views on childhood. — 2 E

Total (30)

*[END OF QUESTION PAPER]*

Official SQA Past Papers: Intermediate 1 English 2005

# X115/102

NATIONAL
QUALIFICATIONS
2005

FRIDAY, 13 MAY
2.05 PM – 2.50 PM

ENGLISH
INTERMEDIATE 1
Critical Essay

Answer **one** question only.

Each question is worth 25 marks.

SAB X115/102 6/11870

Answer ONE question only, taken from any of the Sections A to E. Write the number of the question you attempt in the margin of your answer book.

In all Sections you may use Scottish texts.

You should remember:

- your answer should be relevant to the question
- you should check your spelling and punctuation.

### SECTION A—DRAMA

1. Choose a play in which there is a conflict between two people or groups.

   **Explain why the conflict arose. Go on to show what happens to the people concerned and say whether you think the outcome is satisfactory.**

   In your answer you should refer to such features as: character, plot, or any other appropriate feature.

2. Choose a character from a play who changes during the course of the play.

   **Explain what causes him or her to change and say what effect this change has later on in the play.**

   In your answer you should refer to such features as: character, key scene, or any other appropriate feature.

### SECTION B—PROSE

3. Choose a novel **or** short story in which one of the main characters has to make a decision.

   **Explain what the decision is and show how it is important for the rest of the story.**

   In your answer you should refer to such features as: turning point, character, or any other appropriate feature.

4. Choose a novel **or** a short story **or** a piece of non-fiction **or** a group of prose texts which deals with a subject which interests you, or amuses you, or makes you sad.

   **Say what the subject is and why it has aroused this feeling in you.**

   In your answer you should refer to such features as: the ideas, character, plot, or any other appropriate feature.

### SECTION C—POETRY

5. Choose a poem which describes a place or an incident.

   **What does the poem tell you about the place or incident? How does the language used by the poet help to give you a clear picture of the place or incident?**

   In your answer you should refer to such features as: content, word choice, imagery, or any other appropriate feature.

6. Choose a poem in which there is someone for whom you feel sympathy.

   **Explain why you feel sympathetic towards the person, and what particular words and phrases the poet has used which make you feel this way.**

   In your answer you should refer to such features as: word choice, imagery, or any other appropriate feature.

## SECTION D—MASS MEDIA

7. Choose a film or TV drama* which involves conflict.

   **Describe ONE sequence in the film or TV drama which shows the conflict in action and say how successful you think it is in holding the audience's attention.**

   In your answer you should refer to such features as: use of camera, music, editing, or any other appropriate feature.

8. Choose a film or TV drama* which deals with family life.

   **Briefly describe the family and go on to show how your interest in their lives is kept going.**

   In your answer you should refer to such features as: character, setting, cliffhanger, or any other appropriate feature.

   *"TV drama" may be a single play, series or serial.

## SECTION E—LANGUAGE

9. Consider **one** of the modern ways of communication such as e-mail or texting.

   **What are the differences between this new way of communicating and the older ones—writing letters, for example?**

   In your answer you should refer to such features as: abbreviations, spelling, punctuation, or any other appropriate feature.

10. Consider the language used to persuade you to support a charity or to join in a campaign to take more care of your health.

    **Give examples of the kind of language used and say how successful it is in persuading you.**

    In your answer you should refer to such features as: word choice, tone, or any other appropriate feature.

*[END OF QUESTION PAPER]*

[BLANK PAGE]

2006 | Intermediate I

[BLANK PAGE]

# X115/101

NATIONAL
QUALIFICATIONS
2006

FRIDAY, 12 MAY
1.00 PM – 1.45 PM

ENGLISH
INTERMEDIATE 1
Close Reading

Answer all questions.

30 marks are allocated to this paper.

Read the passage carefully and then answer **all** the questions, **using your own words where asked to do so**.

The questions will ask you to show that:

you understand **what** the writer has said (main ideas and supporting details) (**Understanding—U**);

you can identify **how** the writer has said it (techniques of structure and style) (**Analysis—A**);

you can comment on **how well** the writer has achieved his purpose (using appropriate evidence) (**Evaluation—E**).

A code letter (U, A, E) is used alongside each question to identify its purpose for you.

*This passage is an adapted extract from a chapter of the autobiography of the late actor Christopher Reeve, who played Superman in the film series and was later paralysed after a riding accident.*

## AN AMERICAN FAMILY

When I was born in September 1952, my father, Franklin, was only twenty-four. Although our relationship was always complex—and became increasingly complicated as I moved into adulthood—as a youngster I delighted in the fact that he was young too. Because he was a college professor, first at Columbia, then at Wesleyan and Yale, his
5 vacations generally coincided with ours. My brother, Ben, and I, my half-brothers Brock and Mark, and my half-sister, Alison, all cherished his attention and the activities we shared with him when we were very young.

During the Christmas holidays he taught us to ski. He and my stepmother, Helen, bought a tiny cottage in Ludlow, Vermont, close to several ski areas. All five children
10 were on the slopes by age three and skiing on our own by four or five. Once we were on top of the mountain we waited together as my father stationed himself a hundred yards below. When he was ready we skied down to him one at a time until we were all assembled for his review. Then he would go another hundred yards down the slope and we would repeat the process until we reached the bottom.

15 He had a special talent for communicating with each child based on age and skill. I was the oldest and Mark was the youngest, a difference of nearly ten years, with the others spaced fairly evenly in between. For all of us, a word of praise could make our day. On the other hand, because he thought the lift tickets (about $10) were outrageously expensive, we had to be the first ones on the mountain and the last to leave, which could
20 make for a miserable day. Once the tickets were bought we *skied*, weather and snow conditions notwithstanding, with a thirty-minute break for the bathroom and lunch. (I don't recall any of us ever complaining about the cold or asking to go in early for a cup of hot chocolate.) But we all became expert skiers; Alison qualified to be an instructor when she was only fifteen. Today, in our forties, we are still avid skiers (except me) and
25 have passed our enthusiasm on to our children.

In the springs and summers of our childhood, Pa taught us to swim, sail, play tennis, and paddle a canoe properly—at around nine we all learned to execute a proper J-stroke, which enables one person to keep the canoe going forward in a straight line. Some of these skills were acquired at my grandmother's lakeshore house in the Pocono
30 Mountains of Pennsylvania, others on the Connecticut River and Long Island Sound. As we grew older, we developed special interests in addition to learning the basics. Somehow Pa found time to work and play with each of us individually. Ben was fascinated by all things mechanical and electrical, so he and my father spent hours maintaining the car, an old secondhand Peugeot. As far as I remember, it never went to
35 the shop: they repaired faulty wiring, adjusted the brakes, replaced worn shock absorbers, and gave it routine tune-ups as needed.

Mark liked baseball and beachcombing. He and Pa used to sneak up into the attic, where the old black-and-white television lived in exile, to watch the Yankees. (The TV was not allowed in the living room as a precaution against bad habits.) Down in the basement
40 the two of them created a museum where the most interesting rocks and seashells collected on cruises from Connecticut to Maine were on display.

Alison (always called Alya) and Brock were very musical. Both played the piano, and Alya played the flute as well. Pa played the recorder. Visitors who dropped by in the late afternoon or after dinner were often drawn into the house by the
45 sound of them playing together. Brock and Alya both took riding lessons when they were still quite young. Alya eventually lost interest, but Brock carried on and still rides today. Although he wasn't a rider himself, my father used to drive them to the stables, where he watched with a critical eye at ringside as they worked with their instructor. When Alya dropped out and Brock progressed into show
50 jumping, riding became a unique part of his relationship with our father.

My special interest was the theater. As a youngster I did well in skiing, sailing, and tennis. But by the time I was fourteen, I spent my summers first in acting workshops, then as a theater apprentice, and before long, on tour in a play or performing as a member of a repertory company. Pa generally liked my work.
55 His review after a show was usually kind and constructive: he was the first to point out that I often stood on stage with my knees hyperextended, which made me look tense and inhibited natural movement. After a performance of *The Complaisant Lover*, an obscure English drawing-room comedy in which I attempted to play an upper-class gentleman in his forties (I was seventeen at the
60 time), he approved of my accent but pointed out that I obviously had no idea how to smoke a cigarette, which would be second nature for my character. However, my comic timing received high marks.

No one in our family had ever been an actor, which made me feel truly unique. Pa particularly enjoyed productions in theaters not too far from the water so he could
65 get there on *Pandion*, our twenty-six-foot Pearson sloop. That worked out pretty well: one summer I worked in Boston, another in Boothbay, Maine, and one tour played in four theaters on Cape Cod. It wasn't until I left postgraduate studies at Juilliard and entered the commercial world of film and television that acting became a source of contention between us. As a pure academic, he cherished the
70 theater as a place for language and ideas. He was never very interested in film, even as an art form, and had nothing but contempt for television (except as an outlet for the Yankees).

I'm very grateful that he supported me as I began to learn my trade, and that, for a time, we shared something unique. Without his encouragement in the early
75 years I don't know if I would have developed the self-confidence to attempt such a challenging career.

Adapted from *Nothing is Impossible—Reflections on a new life*,
by Christopher Reeve

## QUESTIONS

*Marks Code*

1. When Christopher Reeve was born, his father "was only twenty-four" (line 1).

    (a) Write down **one** word from the first paragraph (lines 1–7) which tells us that Christopher took pleasure from this. — 1 U/A

    (b) Explain **in your own words** why Christopher's father was able to spend so much time with his children. — 2 U

2. (a) Give **three** reasons why "All five children" (line 9) were good skiers when they were children. — 3 U

    (b) Look at the sentence "When he was ready we skied down to him one at a time until we were all assembled for his review." (lines 12–13)

    Choose any single word or expression in this sentence, and explain what it suggests about the relationship between father and children at this point. — 2 A

3. Explain why "On the other hand" (lines 17–18) works as a link between the sentence it starts and the previous one. — 2 A/E

4. (a) **In your own words**, give **two** reasons why the Reeve children could sometimes be "miserable" (line 20) when they were skiing. — 2 U

    (b) Christopher writes that his family were "avid" (line 24) skiers.

    Write down the word from the same sentence which helps you to understand the meaning of "avid". — 1 U/A

5. Explain fully the purpose of the words after the dash in line 27 (from "at around nine" to "in a straight line"). — 2 A

6. Explain what is suggested by "Somehow" in line 32. — 1 U/A

7. Why does the author use a colon (:) in line 35? — 2 A

8. Christopher writes that his brother and father used to like "to watch the Yankees" (line 38) on television. Select any single word or expression in lines 37–39, and explain how it suggests that this activity was not approved of. — 2 A

9. What does the expression "drawn into" (line 44) suggest about the effect of the music? — 1 U/A

10. Christopher writes about his father's "review after a show" (line 55).

    (a) Show how the rest of the paragraph develops the idea of a "review". — 2 U

    (b) Show why "kind" is an appropriate word to describe his father's "review" of Christopher's performance in *The Complaisant Lover* (line 58). — 2 A/E

11. Why is the comment "except as an outlet for the Yankees" (lines 71–72) effective in its context? Your answer should deal **either** with the tone **or** with the structure of the passage. — 2 E

12. Explain how effective you find the final paragraph as a conclusion to the extract as a whole. — 2 E

13. Christopher Reeve was an American. Identify any **one** expression **apart from place names or people's names** which shows that the passage is in American English. — 1 A

Total (30)

[END OF QUESTION PAPER]

# X115/102

NATIONAL
QUALIFICATIONS
2006

FRIDAY, 12 MAY
2.05 PM – 2.50 PM

ENGLISH
INTERMEDIATE 1
Critical Essay

Answer **one** question only.

Each question is worth 25 marks.

Answer ONE question only, taken from any of the Sections A to E.

In all Sections you may use Scottish texts.

Write the number of the question in the margin of your answer booklet.

The following will be assessed:

- the relevance of your essay to the question you have chosen
- your understanding of the main points of the text(s) through some reference to the relevant areas of content
- your explanation of the ways in which aspects of structure/style/language contribute to the meaning/effect/impact of the chosen text(s)
- your personal reaction to the content or style of the text(s) supported by some textual reference
- the quality and technical accuracy of your writing.

Each question is worth 25 marks.

## SECTION A—DRAMA

*Answers to questions in this section should refer to such relevant features as: conflict, character, key scene(s), theme, plot . . .*

1. Choose a play in which one of the characters has to cope with family **or** school problems.

   What are the problems and how does the character try to deal with them?

2. Choose a play which interests you right from the beginning.

   Say what happens at the beginning and how the characters in the play keep you interested right to the end.

## SECTION B—PROSE

*Answers to questions in this section should refer to such relevant features as: content, character, theme, imagery . . .*

3. Choose a novel **or** short story which you feel has a satisfactory ending.

   Briefly say what happens in the story and then show why you felt that the ending was satisfactory.

4. Choose one or more prose texts (fiction or non-fiction) about a person **or** place that interests you.

   Say what happens to the person or describe the place and explain how the writer makes the person or the place interesting.

## SECTION C—POETRY

*Answers to questions in this section should refer to such relevant features as: content, word choice, theme, imagery . . .*

5. Choose a poem which makes you feel happy **or** sad **or** angry.

   Say what the poem is about and why it makes you feel happy or sad or angry. What particular words or phrases in the poem make you feel that way?

6. Choose a poem which deals with an exciting **or** interesting event.

   Say what the poem is about and go on to show what particular words or phrases or other techniques make it exciting or interesting.

## SECTION D—FILM AND TV DRAMA

*Answers to questions in this section should refer to such relevant features as: character, use of camera, key sequence, editing, sound/music, plot, setting . . .*

7. Choose a film or TV drama* which deals with something supernatural, such as ghosts **or** demons **or** hauntings.

   Give a brief account of what happens and show how the techniques of the film or TV drama help to create a scary or mysterious atmosphere.

8. Choose a film or TV drama* which is mainly about people in a police station, **or** in a hospital, **or** in a city area, **or** in the country.

   Briefly say what the film or TV drama is about and then show how ONE of the characters is very important in keeping your interest.

   *"TV drama" includes a single play, a series or a serial.

[Turn over

## SECTION E—LANGUAGE

*Answers to questions in this section should refer to such relevant features as: vocabulary, accent, dialect, tone, abbreviation, register . . .*

9. Consider the language used by **two** different age groups, for example, young children, teenagers, adults or older people.

    What are the differences you have noticed in how your two groups speak? What reasons are there for the differences?

10. Consider the language used in persuading you to buy particular items such as food, games, DVDs or any other products you might be interested in.

    Choose TWO examples of this kind of advertising and by looking closely at the language show how it is meant to persuade you.

*[END OF QUESTION PAPER]*

2007 | Intermediate I

[BLANK PAGE]

# X115/101

NATIONAL
QUALIFICATIONS
2007

FRIDAY, 11 MAY
1.00 PM – 1.45 PM

# ENGLISH
INTERMEDIATE 1
Close Reading

Answer all questions.

30 marks are allocated to this paper.

Read the passage carefully and then answer **all** the questions, **using your own words where asked to do so**.

The questions will ask you to show that:

you understand **what** the writer has said (main ideas and supporting details) (**Understanding—U**);

you can identify **how** the writer has said it (techniques of structure and style) (**Analysis—A**);

you can comment on **how well** the writer has achieved his purpose (using appropriate evidence) (**Evaluation—E**).

A code letter (U, A, E) is used alongside each question to identify its purpose for you.

*In this passage, the writer describes an amusing incident when his dog is taken to the vet. The "Mrs Harper" he refers to is his wife.*

## AT THE VET

Mrs Harper has a theory that men are big bairns when it comes to pain, even the big bruisers among us.

I think this is a foul slur on Scottish manhood. I believe that wives throughout the northern half of Scotland are well aware of how uncomplainingly we men bear pain or discomfort; how unfazed we are by the prospect of a visit to the doctor's surgery or the hospital, and how reluctant we are to take to our beds, even when suffering horrendous illness.

Mrs Harper's theory is not limited to human males. She says she has amassed plenty of evidence that the males of any species are gey peer craiters when it comes to needles, knives or rubber gloves. What happened last Saturday afternoon, I have to concede, lent weight to her theory.

The two of us and the dog (male) had gone out for our usual weekend walk, timing it between bursts of rain. As we passed the vet's surgery on the way to the riverside park, Mrs Harper noticed that the surgery door was open and remembered suddenly that the big red beast was due his regular dose of kennel-cough medicine.

Seeing her chance, she bustled across the road. All seemed reasonably clear, so she asked if she might make an appointment. The vet proposed getting it over and done with at that moment, as he appeared to have a minor lull between one four-legged emergency and another, so she appeared back outside the surgery door and beckoned me from across the road.

The dog, who had spent the short time we had waited by sizing up the surgery and slowly recalling an assortment of needles, thermometers and rubber-glove smells, showed an unusual reluctance to rise from his sitting position.

Persuaded across the road, he arrived in the surgery and went daft. The vet must have thought he was thoroughly undisciplined, which is untrue. It's just that the assortment of smells in a vet's surgery must be the equivalent of those in a soap shop to a small boy.

He did as he was told and sat, but with his behind and paws quivering on the lino, and his head craning through 270 degrees.

The vet went off to charge the syringe with the medicine, turning his back to the dog while he did so. Those of you who are familiar with dogs will know that a kennel-cough dose is administered not through a needle, but through a blunt squirter up the animal's nostrils.

Our normally placid beast has an abiding horror of this. Mrs Harper says this is not because it's a particularly traumatic procedure or that any vet has been rough with him in the past. It's just that he's male and, consequently, affa feart for himsel.

As the vet turned round, brandishing the blunt-nosed syringe, all pretence of canine discipline vanished.

In the middle of this confusion, with the dog's lead twining my legs and the lino being gouged to destruction as he tried to head for the door, the vet looked at me. "Could you sit down and hold him between your knees to try to steady him?" he said. "Then put your arms round him to lock him while I try to get close."

Not sure that my joints were up to such contortions and exertion, I made to sit down on the nearest seat, as I had been told. Just in time, Mrs Harper pointed out that the seat in question was on castors.

While that might not have been very dignified, look on the bright side: I could have broken the office-chair land-speed record and earned my place in history.

I opted for another seat—sturdy, mahogany—sitting against another wall, and I shochled across, rebelling dog in tow, plonked myself down, hauled him to sit between my knees and locked my arm under his chin.

He calmed momentarily while the vet slipped a nylon muzzle on him. Our dog hasn't so much as nipped anyone in his four years, but it's always best to be cautious in trauma.

The vet tilted the dog's head back and bore down with the syringe. To say that what followed was akin to a whirlwind of dervishes and banshees breaking loose would be gross understatement. I've seen spin-driers and pneumatic drills with less vigour.

Had I not been involved myself, I would not have believed that so much struggling could come from a normally placid and passive beast.

As for the vet, it is difficult to aim for two nostrils when they are thrashing from left to right, despite the animal's owner's best efforts to steady them.

However, the vet managed a quick squirt up one tunnel and half a squirt up the other, which he declared sufficient.

But it didn't end there.

Just as the vet leaned back and slipped the muzzle off the dog, the dog tilted his head back, glowered up into my face and let rip the most enormous sneeze, blowing half his kennel-cough medicine back over me. Having exacted his revenge, he stepped from the surgery as bright and lively as ever. I, meanwhile, had a thumping headache within 15 minutes.

While the dog leaped and bounded and gambolled happily about the riverside park, having forgotten all about his medical encounter just minutes before, my mouth had gone dry, the sky had gone dark and my throat had begun to burn.

Heaven knows what is the active ingredient in kennel-cough serum but, trust me, you don't want to tangle with it.

The headache, dryness and hazy vision persisted for the rest of that evening, despite Mrs Harper's conviction that I was malingering.

Happily, I felt fine after a night's sleep, and the symptoms were but a faint memory by the time I took my place at the kitchen table with my bran flakes the following morning.

Indeed, I'm almost back to normal. The appetite has returned. I'm sleeping well. Best of all, I can now go to kennels nationwide without fear of catching so much as a tickly throat.

Mrs Harper says that she has never seen me looking so healthy in all the time we have been married.

If only I could stop chasing rabbits.

Adapted from *Fortnights* by Norman Harper

## QUESTIONS

*Marks Code*

1. "Men are big bairns when it comes to pain" (line 1). Explain what Mrs Harper means by this.  **2 U**

2. The writer uses humour in the second paragraph (lines 3–7). **Quote** an example.  **1 A**

3. Explain what the writer means by "lent weight to her theory" (lines 10–11).  **2 U**

4. What gave Mrs Harper her "chance" (line 16)?  **1 U**

5. Explain **in your own words** why the vet could treat the dog "at that moment" (line 18).  **1 U**

6. Look at the expression "the equivalent of those in a soap shop to a small boy" (line 26).

    Explain fully how well this illustrates the "smells in a vet's surgery" (line 26) from the dog's point of view.  **2 A/E**

7. Look at lines 27–28.

    **In your own words** explain **one** way in which the dog showed unease or restlessness.  **1 U**

8. What is surprising about the writer's choice of the word "squirter" (line 31) to describe the piece of veterinary equipment?  **1 A**

9. Explain what "normally placid" (line 33) suggests about the dog's nature.  **2 U**

10. "All pretence of canine discipline vanished" (lines 36–37).

    Choose **one** expression in the following paragraph (lines 38–41), and explain how it continues this idea.  **2 A**

11. Explain why the writer chose "another seat" (line 47) to use when holding the dog.  **1 U**

12. Look at the writer's description of what followed the vet's approach to the dog (lines 53–56).

    Choose **one** expression in these lines and explain why it is effective in describing the scene which followed.  **2 A**

13. Look at lines 61–62. Explain fully how any **one** example of the writer's **word choice** helps to emphasise that the writer was unconvinced that the vet had done the job properly.  **2 A**

14. Explain why "But it didn't end there" (line 63) provides an effective link at this stage in the passage.  **3 E**

15. What is surprising about the expressions "glowered" (line 65) and "exacted his revenge" (lines 66–67) as they are used here?  **2 A**

16. Look at the writer's description of what happened after the episode at the vet's surgery (lines 69–71).

    **Quote two** expressions from these lines which help to point out the **contrast** between the dog and the writer.  **2 U/A**

17. Explain why the final paragraph (line 84) is an effective conclusion to the passage.  **2 E**

18. The writer uses some Scots expressions in this piece. Explain how these affected your enjoyment of the passage.  **1 E**

[END OF QUESTION PAPER]

Total **(30)**

# X115/102

NATIONAL
QUALIFICATIONS
2007

FRIDAY, 11 MAY
2.05 PM – 2.50 PM

ENGLISH
INTERMEDIATE 1
Critical Essay

Answer **one** question only.

Each question is worth 25 marks.

Answer ONE question only, taken from any of the Sections A to E.

In all Sections you may use Scottish texts.

Write the number of the question in the margin of your answer booklet.

The following will be assessed:

- the relevance of your essay to the question you have chosen
- your understanding of the main points of the text(s) through some reference to the relevant areas of content
- your explanation of the ways in which aspects of structure/style/language contribute to the meaning/effect/impact of the chosen text(s)
- your personal reaction to the content or style of the text(s) supported by some textual reference
- the quality and technical accuracy of your writing.

Each question is worth 25 marks.

## SECTION A—DRAMA

*Answers to questions in this section should refer to such relevant features as: conflict, character, key scene(s), theme, plot . . .*

1. Choose a play in which a main character has to face a problem.

    Say what the problem is and then go on to show whether you think the character was successful in dealing with the problem in the rest of the play.

2. Choose a play which has an exciting **or** a sad **or** a happy ending.

    Briefly say what happens in the play, and then, in more detail, describe the ending and say why you felt it was exciting **or** sad **or** happy.

## SECTION B—PROSE

*Answers to questions in this section should refer to such relevant features as: content, character, theme, imagery . . .*

3. Choose a novel **or** short story in which a character gains your sympathy because of the situation he or she is in at one point in the novel or short story.

    Say what the situation is and how the character deals with it. Go on to explain why you feel sympathy for him or her.

4. Choose a prose text (fiction or non-fiction) which you enjoyed because of its interesting theme **or** character(s) **or** setting.

    Describe the theme **or** character(s) **or** setting and show how the writer has made the text interesting to you.

## SECTION C—POETRY

*Answers to questions in this section should refer to such relevant features as: content, word choice, theme, imagery . . .*

5. Choose a poem which tells the story of an incident.

    Briefly tell the story and go on to show how the language of the poem gives you a clear understanding of what happens.

6. Choose a poem which deals with a person who interests you.

    Briefly say what the poem is about and go on to show how the poet uses particular words and phrases to make the person interesting.

## SECTION D—FILM AND TV DRAMA

*Answers to questions in this section should refer to such relevant features as: character, use of camera, key sequence, editing, sound/music, plot, setting . . .*

7. Choose a film or TV drama* where the opening sequence creates a particular atmosphere which is important for the whole film or TV drama.

    Say what the atmosphere is and why it is important. Go on to show how the atmosphere is created by the techniques of film or television.

8. Choose a film or TV drama* which deals with a crisis in the life of a family, **or** a town, **or** a country, **or** a planet.

    Describe the crisis and show how the film director or the programme makers have used the techniques of film or television to make it exciting and dramatic.

*"TV drama" includes a single play, a series or a serial.

**[Turn over**

## SECTION E—LANGUAGE

*Answers to questions in this section should refer to such relevant features as: vocabulary, accent, dialect, tone, abbreviation, register . . .*

9. Consider the language used by any particular group of people to talk about their particular interest—their job, their hobby, their sport, their music, for example.

    Give some examples of the special terms they use when talking to others in their group. Why do you think these terms are used and how useful do you think these special terms are?

10. Consider the language of advertising on TV **or** on the Internet **or** in magazines.

    Choose one advertisement (or more than one) and explain which aspects of the advertisement(s) you find most successful and which aspect you find least successful.

*[END OF QUESTION PAPER]*

**2008** | Intermediate I

[BLANK PAGE]

**X115/101**

NATIONAL
QUALIFICATIONS
2008

THURSDAY, 15 MAY
1.00 PM – 1.45 PM

ENGLISH
INTERMEDIATE 1
Close Reading

Answer all questions.

30 marks are allocated to this paper.

Read the passage carefully and then answer **all** the questions, **using your own words where asked to do so**.

The questions will ask you to show that:

> you understand **what** the writer has said (main ideas and supporting details) (**Understanding—U**);
>
> you can identify **how** the writer has said it (techniques of structure and style) (**Analysis—A**);
>
> you can comment on **how well** the writer has achieved his purpose (using appropriate evidence) (**Evaluation—E**).

A code letter (U, A, E) is used alongside each question to identify its purpose for you.

*In this passage, the writer tells us about a famous Scottish mystery.*

# THE ISLAND OF LOST SOULS

Seven lumps of rock 30 miles off the west coast of Lewis, the outermost of the Outer Hebrides, the Flannan Islands have a good claim to be the most deserted place in Britain. The only inhabitants are thousands of puffins, some nesting fulmars, the "little people" of Gaelic folklore and the ghosts. But I have longed to visit the Flannans ever since, when I was a little boy, my father would scare us into delighted terror with the story of the Flannan lighthouse, one of the strangest unsolved mysteries in Scottish history.

The story goes like this: for centuries the Seven Hunters, as the local people called the islands, had preyed on shipping. Innumerable vessels had perished on the rocks, including remnants of the Spanish Armada. So the Victorians, with the spirit typical of the age, decided to build a lighthouse here, on the edge of the world.

A year after the lighthouse was lit, a steamer from Oban was sent out to relieve the three lighthouse keepers, who had been on the island, alone, for three months. As the ship approached in the morning gloom, her master could see no lights on the island. Captain Harvie sent two men scrambling up the cliff. The gate to the lighthouse enclosure was bolted, but the door of the lighthouse itself was open. Food lay uneaten on the table. Two sets of boots and oilskins had gone, but the third was still in the rack. The entries in the lighthouse log ended abruptly a week earlier, and the clocks had wound down. A chair lay on its back, but otherwise there was no sign of violence. The lamp was filled with paraffin, and the beds were neatly made. Of the three lighthouse keepers there was not a sign. The mystery remains unsolved, though many have put forward theories. For more than 30 years I had wanted to see the place for myself.

We anchored at the main island, Eilean Mor, with the lighthouse silhouetted above us through the clearing mist. Most of the steps in the side of the rock have been worn away by the sea, and all that remains of the handrail are a few rusting posts. We had to time our jump to the height of the 5 foot swell, and cling to the seaweed. We crawled up the side of the rock, 80 feet of scramble, to emerge on the top of the cliff. There a reception committee was waiting, clad in formal evening wear: several thousand tiny puffins stood and stared at us, curious, entirely without fear.

The lighthouse has been fully automated since the Seventies, when the last keepers departed, leaving the islands in perfect human isolation, save for the helicopter that lands once a year for the annual service by the Northern Lighthouse Board, and the odd rugged birdwatcher.

The sense of solitude was as penetrating as the mist. Here on the last outcrop of the Atlantic shelf, look in any direction and you see . . . nothing. Solitude brought St Flannan here in the first place. Below the lighthouse is the ruin of his "chapel", the tiny stone bothy where this resilient hermit reputedly spent several years in the 9th century. We crawled inside; the rising wind howled through the cracks between the stones. What must it have been like for the lighthouse keepers, cooped up in a brick tube for months, battered by wind, rain and waves? That was one of the many questions asked by Superintendent Robert Muirhead, who was dispatched by the Northern Lighthouse Board in January, 1901, to try to solve the Flannan Islands mystery.

Muirhead studied the weather, the tides, and the logs of every ship in the area. He interviewed the families of the vanished men, the people of Lewis and the ocean.
A man of the modern age, an engineer, Muirhead was plunged into a world of ancient superstitions.

Some claimed that the men had been devoured by sea monsters, or spirited away by the angry spirit of Flannan. The poet Wilfred Wilson Gibson whipped up controversy by writing a ghostly poem imagining that the men had turned into three great black birds, and plunged into the sea. Newspapers luridly speculated that the men had fallen out, or been driven to madness and suicide by solitude, or the demon drink; it was rumoured that one man had murdered the other two, and then hurled himself from the cliff-top. The sailors and fishermen talked of the "Fist of God", the freak wave of ancient maritime legend, a rogue wall of water that rises suddenly out of the sea and pulls down ships and men, only to vanish again.

Several aspects of the incident did not (and do not) add up. The superintendent dismissed the notion that the three men had been blown off the island by a mighty gust of wind, pointing out that since the wind was westerly that night, this would have forced them up to the island and away from the cliffs. About 100 feet above sea-level, safety railings had been wrenched out of shape. Muirhead reckoned a boulder must have crashed down from the ledge above, but the sight of the ironwork—"displaced and twisted in a manner difficult to believe unless actually seen"—spooked even him. Why had one of the men left the lighthouse building in his shirtsleeves? If some catastrophe had befallen the men, who had had time to bolt the entrance gate to the lighthouse? Above all, if the men had drowned, the prevailing tides should have swept the bodies towards the Hebrides. Despite an intensive search, no body was found.

We stood on the crumbling steps leading down to the north landing. Here the wind was so strong that it was easy to imagine a man being swept to his death from here; but three? Was there some tragic collision between new technology and ancient beliefs? Or was there a rational explanation? Muirhead concluded "that an unexpectedly large roller had come up on the Island, and swept them away with resistless force".

He was probably right. Recent satellite research has shown that rogue waves of immense height are a more frequent occurrence than previously believed, scientific fact rather than maritime folklore.

Ben Macintyre in *The Times Magazine*, 21st January, 2006 (slightly adapted)

## QUESTIONS

*Marks Code*

1. Explain why "the Flannan Islands have a good claim to be the most deserted place in Britain" (lines 2–3).

   **Use your own words** as far as possible.    2 U

2. What is surprising about the expression "delighted terror" (line 5)?    1 A

3. Why is the word "preyed" (line 9) appropriate here?    2 A

4. Look at lines 15–21, and explain **in your own words** what the "mystery" was.    2 U

5. Look at lines 24–27.

   Explain why any **one** example of the writer's **word choice** effectively makes it clear that the climb up to the lighthouse was a difficult one.    2 E

6. Look at the words "formal evening wear" (line 28).

   Explain why this expression may seem **either** surprising **or** appropriate here.    2 A

7. Choose an expression from lines 30–33, and show how it helps us to understand the meaning of "rugged" as it is used here.    2 U

8. The writer tells us: "The sense of solitude was as penetrating as the mist" (line 34).

   (i) What does the writer mean by a "sense of solitude"?    1 U

   (ii) Why is this an effective comparison or simile?    2 E

9. Why does the writer use inverted commas round "chapel" (line 36)?    1 A

10. Show how **one** example of the writer's **word choice** in lines 38–40 effectively conveys the hardships of the lighthouse keepers' lives.    2 E

11. What do lines 43–44 tell us about the way Muirhead approached his task?    1 U

12. Look at the sentence "A man of the modern age, an engineer, Muirhead was plunged into a world of ancient superstitions" (lines 45–46).

    How does one feature of the **imagery** help to suggest something about Muirhead's task?    2 A

13. Write down an expression from the next paragraph which continues the idea introduced by "superstitions" (line 46).    1 U

14. Show how the meaning of "luridly speculated" (line 50) is made clear in the rest of the paragraph.    2 A

15. Look at lines 57–68.

    Identify **two** of the "aspects" of the events which "do not . . . add up".

    **Use your own words** as far as possible.    2 U

16. Identify one feature of **sentence structure** in lines 69–72 which is appropriate for this story of mystery.    1 A

17. Explain why any feature of the final paragraph (lines 75–77) helps to make these sentences a satisfying conclusion to the passage.    2 E

**Total (30)**

*[END OF QUESTION PAPER]*

# X115/102

NATIONAL
QUALIFICATIONS
2008

THURSDAY, 15 MAY
2.05 PM – 2.50 PM

ENGLISH
INTERMEDIATE 1
Critical Essay

Answer **one** question only.

Each question is worth 25 marks.

Answer ONE question only, taken from any of the Sections A to E.

In all Sections you may use Scottish texts.

Write the number of the question in the margin of your answer booklet.

The following will be assessed:

- the relevance of your essay to the question you have chosen
- your understanding of the main points of the text(s) through some reference to the relevant areas of content
- your explanation of the ways in which aspects of structure/style/language contribute to the meaning/effect/impact of the chosen text(s)
- your personal reaction to the content or style of the text(s) supported by some textual reference
- the quality and technical accuracy of your writing.

**Each question is worth 25 marks.**

## SECTION A—DRAMA

*Answers to questions in this section should refer to such relevant features as: conflict, character, key scene(s), theme, plot . . .*

1. Choose a play in which there is an important relationship between two of the characters.

    Identify the relationship and go on to show how it develops and why, in your opinion, it is important in the play as a whole.

2. Choose a play which deals with an unpleasant aspect of life.

    Show how the unpleasant aspect of life affects one or more of the characters in the play and say whether you sympathise with the character(s) or not.

## SECTION B—PROSE

*Answers to questions in this section should refer to such relevant features as: content, character, theme, imagery . . .*

3. Choose a novel **or** short story which has an important turning point.

    Say how the turning point was reached and go on to show how it affects the characters and the ending of the story.

4. Choose a novel **or** a short story **or** a piece of non-fiction which deals with a topic **or** a character **or** a place which interests you.

    Describe the topic **or** the character **or** the place and show how the writer makes it interesting for you.

## SECTION C—POETRY

*Answers to questions in this section should refer to such relevant features as: content, word choice, theme, imagery, sound . . .*

5. Choose a poem about a person who has to face difficulties or problems.

    Say what the poem is about and show how the writer uses particular words and phrases to help you to sympathise with the person.

6. Choose a poem which creates an exciting **or** dramatic **or** sad atmosphere.

    Say what the poem is about and go on to show what particular words or phrases help to create the atmosphere.

## SECTION D—FILM AND TV DRAMA

*Answers to questions in this section should refer to such relevant features as: character, use of camera, key sequence(s), editing, sound/music, plot, setting . . .*

7. Choose a film with an opening sequence which captures your interest.

    Say what interests you in the sequence and show how the sequence made a good beginning to the film as a whole.

8. Choose a film **or** TV drama* which deals with at least one important relationship.

    Describe the relationship and show how the film or programme makers use the techniques of film or TV drama to keep you interested in the relationship.

*"TV drama" includes a single play, a series or a serial.

## SECTION E—LANGUAGE

*Answers to questions in this section should refer to such relevant features as: vocabulary, accent, dialect, tone, abbreviation, register . . .*

9. Consider the language used in TV programmes targeted at young people.

    Identify some ways in which the language is different from the language used in other television programmes. Why do you think this language is attractive to young people?

10. Consider the language used in advertisements related to some aspect of daily life such as food or drink or leisure pursuits or holidays.

    By referring to specific examples say why you think some aspects of the language used are successful in persuading you to buy the product.

[END OF QUESTION PAPER]

[BLANK PAGE]

[BLANK PAGE]

[BLANK PAGE]

[BLANK PAGE]

# Acknowledgements

Leckie and Leckie is grateful to the copyright holders, as credited, for permission to use their material:
An extract from 'Nothing is Impossible' by Christopher Reeve, published by Century. Reprinted by permission of The Random House Group Ltd (2004 Close Reading pp 2-3);
The Times Magazine for an article 'The Island of Lost Souls' by Ben Macintyre © NI Syndication (2008 Close Reading pp 2-3).

The following companies have very generously given permission to reproduce their copyright material free of charge:
Extract from 'Round Ireland with a Fridge' by Tony Hawks. Reprinted by permission of The Random House Group Limited. (2004 Close Reading paper pp 2-3);
D.C. Thomson & Co. and Aberdeen Journals Ltd for an extract from 'Fortnights' by Norman Harper, published in (2007 Close Reading pp 2-3).

# Intermediate 1 Critical Essay Supplementary Advice

This advice, which is supplementary to the published Performance Criteria, is designed to assist with the placing of scripts within the full range of marks. However, the Performance Criteria as published give the primary definitions. The mark range for each Category is identified.

| IV  8–11 | III  12–15 | II  16–19 | I  20–25 |
|---|---|---|---|
| An essay which falls into this category may do so for a variety of reasons.<br><br>It could be<br><br>• that it fails to achieve the criterion of "mainly accurate"<br><br>• or that any knowledge and understanding of the material is not used to provide a discernible line of thought<br><br>• or that personal reaction/opinion is unconvincing<br><br>• or that discussion of techniques is not sufficiently related to the point being made<br><br>• or that the answer is simply too thin. | **Understanding**<br>• Knowledge of the text(s), and a **basic understanding** of the main point(s) will be used<br><br>to provide a **discernibly relevant** response to the question.<br><br>• Some reference to the relevant **areas of content** will be made in the course of the response. | **Understanding**<br>• Knowledge of the text(s), and an **understanding** of the main point(s) will be used<br><br>to provide a response **generally relevant** to the question.<br><br>• Some reference to the **text(s) or more generally to its content** will be made in the course of the response. | **Understanding**<br>• Knowledge of the text(s), and an **understanding** of the main point(s) or **central concerns** will be used<br><br>to provide a response **relevant** to the question.<br><br>• Some reference to the **text(s) as well as to its content** will be made in the course of the response. |
|  | **Analysis**<br>• There will be a **description** of some obvious techniques which add to the meaning or impact of the text(s). | **Analysis**<br>• An **attempt** will be made **to explain** how some obvious techniques add to the meaning or impact of the text(s). | **Analysis**<br>• There will be an **explanation** of how some obvious techniques add to the meaning or impact of the text(s). |
|  | **Evaluation**<br>• There will be some engagement with the text(s) and a **personal reaction** to it will be stated or implied. | **Evaluation**<br>• There will be some engagement with the text(s) and a **personal opinion** will be stated or implied. | **Evaluation**<br>• There will be some engagement with the text(s) and a **basic evaluation** will be stated or implied. |
|  | **Expression**<br>• Language will convey meaning clearly.<br><br>Spelling, grammar and punctuation are mainly accurate. | **Expression**<br>• Language will convey meaning clearly.<br><br>Spelling, grammar and punctuation are mainly accurate. | **Expression**<br>• Language will convey meaning clearly.<br><br>Spelling, grammar and punctuation are mainly accurate. |

# English Intermediate 1
## 2004 to 2008 Exams
## Critical Essay

**Marking principles for Critical Essay are as follows**

- The essay should first be read to establish whether it achieves success in **all** the Performance Criteria for Grade C, including relevance and the standards for technical accuracy outlined in Note 1 below.
- If minimum standards are not achieved in any **one** or more of the Performance Criteria, the maximum mark which can be awarded is 11.
- If minimum standards have been achieved, then the supplementary marking grids will allow you to place the work on a scale of marks out of 25.
- The Category awarded and the mark should be placed at the end of the essay.

**Notes**

1. *Mainly accurate*
   Although a few errors may be present, spelling, vocabulary and sentence structures will be sufficiently accurate to convey the candidate's meaning at first reading

2. *Using the Category descriptions*
   - Categories are not grades. Although derived from performance criteria at C and the indicators of excellence for Grade A, the four categories are designed primarily to assist with placing each candidate response at an appropriate point on a continuum of achievement. Assumptions about final grades or association of final grades with particular categories should not be allowed to influence objective assessment.
   - Once an essay has been deemed to pass the basic criteria, it does not have to meet all the suggestions for Category II (for example) to fall into that Category. More typically there will be a spectrum of strengths and weaknesses which span categories.

## Grade C
**Performance Criteria**

(a) Understanding
   As appropriate to task, the response demonstrates understanding of the main point(s) of the text(s) through some reference to relevant areas of content.

(b) Analysis
   The response describes some of the more obvious ways in which aspects of structure/style/language contribute to meaning/effect/impact.

(c) Evaluation
   The response contains a stated or implied personal reaction to the content or style of the text(s), supported by some textual reference.

(d) Expression
   Language conveys meaning clearly and a generally relevant line of thought is discernible; spelling, grammar and punctuation are mainly accurate.

It should be noted that the term "text" encompasses printed, audio or film/video text(s) which may be literary (fiction or non-fiction) or may relate to aspects of media or language.

**Language Questions – 9 and 10**

- The "text" which should be dealt with in a language question is the research which the pupil has done. Examples taken from their research must be there for you to see.
- However, to demonstrate understanding and analysis related to these examples there has to be some ability to make comparisons or to group words of similar kinds to make a point about the use of language.

## English Intermediate 1
## 2008
## Close Reading (cont.)

**13.** *Any one from:*
- "(devoured by) sea monsters"
- "spirited away"
- "(the angry) spirit (of Flannan)"
- "ghostly"
- "turned into…birds"

**14.** There are a number of melodramatic/exaggerated/sensational guesses/ideas/possibilities advanced
OR
One example from madness/suicide/drink/murder/freak wave and comment on the fantastic/macabre/grotesque nature of that example
OR
Quotation of "rumoured"
and comment on the sensationalism/non-factual nature of eg murder/suicide
There must be an understanding of luridness or speculation shown by quotation from/reference to elsewhere in the paragraph

**15.**

| Originals | References/paraphrases |
|---|---|
| the wind was westerly that night | direction of the wind |
| The railings…had been wrenched out of shape OR ironwork "displaced and twisted" | Severity/extent of the damage to the iron railings |
| One of the men left…in his shirtsleeves | One man left without putting on a coat |
| Bolt the entrance gate | The gate was locked |
| No body was found | No corpses were washed up (despite direction of tide) |

**16.** (Frequent) use of (unanswered) questions.
Use of semi-colon

**17.** The facts (about big waves) solve the mystery
OR
the mention of rogue waves recaps an idea previously mentioned (the "Fist of God")
OR
"folklore" recaps the idea of superstition previously mentioned
OR
the alliteration of "fact" and "folklore"
OR
the **balance/contrast** of the two phrases "scientific fact" and "maritime folklore" is neat
OR
"he was probably right" briefly/neatly sums up OR provides a comforting tone
OR
The contrast between short and long sentences is neat

## Intermediate English 1
## Critical Essay
## 2008

N.B. Please see pages 7–8 for the Critical Essay Paper

# English Intermediate 1
# 2008
# Close Reading

1. They are remote (gloss of "30 miles off the west coast of Lewis"); They are barren (gloss of "lumps of rock"); They are uninhabited (gloss of "The only inhabitants ...")
   *Any two of the above or one full comment.*

2. The words contradict each other/are unusual with each other/are paradoxical/are an oxymoron.

3. It continues the idea/metaphor/image/personification of "(Seven) Hunters"
   OR
   the idea/metaphor/image/personification of "(Seven) Hunters" is connected with the losses of shipping

4. The lighthouse keepers had vanished
   Suddenly or for no obvious reason
   The men's lives had been disrupted

5. *Any one from:*

   - Steps being "worn away"
     (clearly) showing the danger/perilousness of the ascent

   - "All that remains…are…posts"
     (clearly) shows there was nothing to hold on to

   - "(We had to time our jump to the height of) the 5 ft swell"
     (clearly) shows the (extent of the) danger/how testing it was

   - "cling"
     (clearly) shows how dangerous/taxing it was

   - "cling to the seaweed"
     (clearly) shows the lack of stable/firm handholds

   - "(We) crawled"
     (clearly) shows the slowness of progress
     OR
     how it was impossible to stand upright

   - "80 ft"
     (clearly) shows the length/extent of the task

   - "scramble"
     (clearly) shows the climb to be strenuous/demanding
     OR
     the shifting nature of the ground

6. Surprising:
   it (usually) refers to human clothes
   and here applies to the birds
   OR
   It is associated with (elegant) special occasions
   and the setting is in the wilds

6. continued

   Appropriate:
   it is black and white
   which is the birds' feather colouring
   OR
   The areas of black and white
   look like a jacket and shirt
   OR
   The expression reflects/repeats
   idea of or tone of "reception committee"

7. "The last keepers departed"
   OR
   the island is "in perfect human isolation"
   OR
   "the helicopter (that) lands once a year"
   And so any visitor would have to be hardy/self-sufficient/resilient/strong/robust/able to look after him or herself

8. (i) Feeling of loneliness/being alone/seclusion

   (ii) Just as the mist was unignorable/intrusive
   So the feeling (of loneliness) was strong/unsettling/inescapable

9. To show the vagueness or inappropriateness of the term/it's not really a chapel

10. - "Cooped up"
      (clearly) conveys the crampedness

    - "in a brick tube"
      (clearly) conveys the crampedness
      OR
      the spartan nature of the accommodation

    - "for months"
      (clearly) conveys the long time they had to spend there

    - "battered"
      (clearly) conveys the harshness/severity of the weather

    - "wind, rain and waves"
      (clearly) conveys the multiplicity/variety of hostile elements

11. He was thorough/painstaking/professional/scientific

12. "(Muirhead was) plunged"
    suggests the suddenness/(figurative) depth/overwhelming nature of his task
    OR
    his unpreparedness
    OR
    the (implied) contrast with his usual life

    "world (of ancient superstitions)"
    suggests the size/complexity/range of the old beliefs he came across
    OR
    the (implied) contrast with his usual life.

# English Intermediate 1
## 2007
## Close Reading

1. Men behave like children/are dramatic/are scared when they are unwell/suffering/ill/injured/hurt.

2. *Any one of*
   - "foul slur"
   - "how uncomplainingly …"
   - "how unfazed …"
   - "how reluctant …"
   - "horrendous illness".

3. Backed up/substantiated/endorsed/added to/proved her ideas/her view/what she believed (about men).

4. The vet's door being open.

5. There was a calm period/he wasn't busy (gloss of "lull").

6. Suggests multiplicity/variety/strength of smells AND repulsion or antipathy or association with an unpleasant experience.

7. (Constant) movement of body OR (wide) movements of head (gloss of "quivering" or "caring").

8. It is slang/colloquial/imprecise.

9. He is usually easy-going/docile/calm/composed/disciplined/well-behaved.

10. "confusion" suggests chaos;
    "the dog's lead twining my legs" suggests lack of control;
    "the lino being gouged (to destruction)" suggests (frantic) uncontrolled behaviour;
    "he tried to head for the door" suggests wilfulness on the dog's part;
    the vet's request(s) (to hold/steady/lock the dog) indicate(s) dog is not under control.

11. First seat (was on castors and therefore) would move easily.
    OR
    The second seat was less mobile.

12. *Any one of*
    - "a whirlwind" suggests rapid movement
    - "dervishes" suggests rapid movement
    - "banshees" suggests intensity of noise
    - "gross understatement" suggests great chaos
    - "spin-driers and pneumatic drills with less vigour" suggests (rapidity of) movement
    - "bore down" suggests intimidatory nature of action

13. *Any one of*
    - "quick/squirt" suggests perfunctory quality
    - "half a squirt" suggests lack of thoroughness
    - "declared (sufficient)" suggests/emphasises the writer's reservation.

14. "But" introduces the contrast between the preceding apparent success (referred back to by 'it') and the following drawback (suggested by 'didn't end').

15. They ascribe human powers of emotion to the dog (personification).

16. Ideas are of happiness and misery.
    *Contrast any of*
    - "leaped"
    - "bounded"
    - "gambolled"
    - "happily"
    - "having forgotten all about his medical encounter"
    *with any of*
    - "my mouth had gone dry"
    - "the sky had gone dark"
    - "my throat had begun to burn"

17. Surprise is in keeping with content/events of the passage.
    OR
    Humour is in keeping with the tone of the passage.

18. Either acceptable:
    in favour: (eg) added colour/shades of meaning/couthiness/humour;
    against: (eg) incomprehension because of unfamiliarity.

N.B. Please see pages 7–8 for the Critical Essay Paper

# English Intermediate 1
# 2006
# Close Reading

1. (a) "delighted"

   (b) his holidays happened at the same time as theirs (i.e. gloss of "his vacations generally coincided with ours").

2. (a) *Any three from*:
   Father taught them; house was in a ski area; children started very young; they skied all day.

   (b) "When he was ready" suggests father was in control/dominant; "(we skied down to him) one at a time" suggests discipline; "(for his) review" suggests strictness, propensity for criticism; "(we were all) assembled" suggests discipline/control.

3. It indicates the contrast between the positive/pleasant and the negative/unpleasant. Quotations of "make our day" and "miserable day" acceptable.

4. (a) *Any two from*:
   They had to ski all day
   They had to be oblivious of weather (gloss of "notwithstanding")
   They were given little respite (accept insertion of, e.g. "only" or "just" in answer referring to break as indication of understanding of brevity)

   (b) "enthusiasm"

5. They expand/explain/clarify/exemplify/tell you what is meant by "(paddle a canoe) properly" or what is correct technique, ie lift or gloss.

6. Idea that the father's task was difficult or that this is a considerable/surprising achievement or idea of admiration.

7. What follows the colon is a development/explanation/itemisation of the reasons the car was never sent for repair.

8. *Any one of*:
   - "sneak" having connotation of furtiveness, shame etc;
   - TV being in attic suggests inaccessibility;
   - "in exile" suggests shame, disapproval, pariah quality;
   - "not allowed" suggests a positive decision to ban TV;
   - "precaution" suggests guarding against something;
   - "bad habits" clearly associates TV with undesirable activity.

9. It was attractive/alluring/compelling/made visitors (accept "them") want to come into the house, etc.

10. (a) It consists of/gives (examples of)/points out comments on (aspects of) performance/stagecraft.

    (b) Favourable comment on accent or timing or on some aspects of his performance.

11. Tone: it lightens in context of more serious ideas
    Structure: it relates back to/reminds us of/repeats earlier mentioning of/previous reference to Yankees.

12. Answer should take any idea from the final paragraph (e.g. idea of gratitude/support/apprenticeship/sharing/encouragement) and relate this to a (substantiated) previous instance in the extract.
    It could also relate to an affectionate tone, with an instance from elsewhere cited.
    It could mention use of "unique" echoing use/sense of word (twice) elsewhere in the passage.
    It could also comment on element of affection being surprising, since evidence elsewhere suggests father was something of a martinet.

13. Answer could relate to use/sense of "(college) professor", or "vacations"; to spelling of "theater(s)"; to price of ski ticket in dollars; to reference to baseball/basement/lakeshore; to use of "shop" to mean "garage".

N.B. Please see pages 7–8 for the Critical Essay Paper

# English Intermediate 1
# 2005
# Close Reading

1. Any two from:
   - Poster of footballer
   - Football fixture list
   - Photos of the rugby team
   - Photo of a Ferrari
   - Illuminated globe
   - Model tank
   - Heap of lolly sticks
   - Lack of books.

2. ("there's also a Game Boy in the house) somewhere…"
   "He doesn't mind …"

3. (a) 'But' indicates the contrast between Daniel's eagerness to get out of the house with the writer's reluctance to leave.

   (b) Parenthesis/ to give some additional information/ to indicate a pause.

4. (a) " …( seems rather) less stereotypical …"

   (b) One example from:
   - He has models made by himself or made at school **instead** of coming out of a kit.
   - The heap of lolly sticks is not a mess **but** they are actually the roof for a model house.
   - He has sports posters/fixture lists **but** they are out of date.

5. He is more lively/shows greater interest in (when talking about) things he made himself.
   **or** the priority of his interests is unusual
   **or** he is not a typical boy

6. Evokes a tone of surprise/ disbelief/ shock/ amazement.

7. Horticulture/to earth potatoes/ incubated/ hatched under a lamp.
   The writer makes use of technical terminology (to demonstrate Daniel's knowledge).

8. **Similarities** – two from:
   - They grew up in the same place
   - They went to the same school
   - Walked the same paths
   - Had some of the same teachers.
   
   **Differences:**
   - The writer's parents were doctors not farmers/had different jobs.
   - The writer's childhood home was not as isolated as Daniel's farm.

9. Irrespective of where/how they are brought up children today grow up more quickly and are tougher or more street-wise or more up-to-date or more cynical.

10. To indicate a change in direction/to show that the writer is introducing the other side of the argument.

11. To indicate the titles of films and television programmes.

12. Question and answer style which helps focus on/ draw attention to; what Daniel does/ his activities.

13. Examples of humour are found e.g. in the places where Daniel's answer confounds the writer's expectations e.g.:
    - Daniel's comment about reading books by Enid Blyton – 'Do I know them'? – links with the writer's own thoughts in the first paragraph.
    - The apparently serious answer to the writer asking him if he gets a comic: 'No. But he did used to get 'Poultry News'.'
    - Use of 'Macbeth' as Daniel's example of a 15 certificate film.

14. Effective as it draws together his comparisons of past and present.
    Effective as it presents his conclusion – today's childhood could even be better than that of the past.

N.B. Please see pages 7–8 for the Critical Essay Paper

# Pocket answer section for SQA English Intermediate 1 2004–2008

© 2008 Scottish Qualifications Authority/Leckie & Leckie, All Rights Reserved
Published by Leckie & Leckie Ltd, 3rd Floor, 4 Queen Street, Edinburgh EH2 1JE
tel: 0131 220 6831, fax: 0131 225 9987, enquiries@leckieandleckie.co.uk, www.leckieandleckie.co.uk

## English Intermediate 1
## 2004
## Close Reading

1. One is deliberate/intentional/planned, the other happens by chance.

2. He had to entertain the audience/do a turn/fill the gap while the judging was completed.

3. (a) The song was to be funny and better (than the others)/different (from the others).

   (b) It was much worse/poorer/less funny.

4. **Word choice**
   Now (I consider myself …)/how can I put it?/yes, that's it and explanation – eg addresses reader directly

   **Punctuation**
   Ref. to dashes and explanation – eg indicates hesitation/pause/thought.
   OR ref. to question mark and explanation, eg indicates the writer thinking to himself.

5. By highlighting/emphasising/clarifying/illustrating the lack of care/pride/supervision/assistance.

6. • Recognition/explanation of irony OR sarcasm.
   • It made them seem even more ridiculous.
   • He was making fun of Seamus.

7. **Feature**
   Reference to:
   • colon which introduces examples
   • list of examples
   • dash OR word order emphasising 'all'.

   **Explanation**
   To show nature/number of his audience.

8. (a) They were surprised/astonished.

   (b) He was amazed and embarrassed.

   (c) The (silly) costume wasn't enough/wasn't funny/made them feel stupid.

9. **Word choice**
   ref. to frantic (signals)/flapping (arms)/ brandishing … (in anger)/(looked) accusingly/ paralysed (with nerves) and indication of how this suggests desperation/heightened emotion

   **Sentence structure**
   brevity indicating nervousness/anxiety/filmic technique (cutting from scene to scene)
   OR ref. to use of questions building to a climax/indicating the writer's sense of panic.

10. Brevity of sentence/paragraph on its own/personification (metaphor acceptable)/ alliteration.

11. "… frantic signals." (line 41) OR " … flapping arms …" (line 42)

12. Answers may, for example, refer to the sentence:
    • being summative/rounding off the incident
    • dealing with the happy conclusion to the episode
    • being structured so as to build to a climax
    • bringing together the audience, performers and writer
    • linking to the opening
    • linking to earlier elements.

N.B. Please see pages 7–8 for the Critical Essay Paper